The central panel of the restored East Window, by John Hayward,
depicting Our Lady of Walsingham with the inscription
'Virgo Pia Genetrix Sit Nobis'
Tender Virgin be Our Mother

Walsingham, Parish Church of St. Mary.

A FIRE IN WALSINGHAM

at Saint Mary & All Saints Church,

Little Walsingham

on 14th July 1961

INTRODUCTION

The year 2011 marks the 950th anniversary of Lady Richeldis' vision of the Blessed Virgin Mary. It is also the 50th anniversary of the fire which almost completely destroyed Little Walsingham's Parish Church.

As part of the celebration of the vision and building of the Holy House in Walsingham it was thought appropriate to produce a book about the fire at the church.

Fortunately three box files were found in the Vicarage full to over-flowing with photographs, newspaper cuttings, leaflets, postcards and other information! There were hundreds of pictures of the fire, the ruins, building works and the Consecration Service in 1964. Also, and of great interest, there were photographs of the church before the fire, including the Shrine and statue of Our Lady of Walsingham before it was moved to the current Anglican Shrine in 1931.

The format of this book soon became clear; the difficulty was choosing which images to include, or rather, leave out!

On the day after the fire it is recorded Father Colin Stephenson, Administrator of the Shrine Church, told the Press it was a great catastrophe but he added, *"The church will rise again."*

The photographs in this book show the church before, during and after the fire. The last chapter proves the church has indeed risen again and is alive today. It is appropriate the final image is of Our Lady, as Patron and Protectress, holding the restored church in her arms, rising phoenix-like from the fire.

Just inside S. Mary's is a simple plaque which records the rebuilding of the church after the devastating fire of 1961. Three names are recorded: The Reverend A A Roe Vicar, John Banson and Robin Sayer Churchwardens.

The photographs and memories of 14th July 1961 tell their own story. But what it must have been like for the young vicar, only recently appointed, and his two churchwardens, on the morning after the fire, can only be imagined.

One of the more poignant pictures is of Father Roe celebrating Mass in the ruins of the church with blackened walls and debris strewn around him. He is surrounded by a group of parishioners quietly determined that S. Mary's would rise 'phoenix-like' from the flames of the fire. In those early days the question was seriously asked as to whether the church should be re-built at all or left as a romantic ruin! However, the Wardens and PCC appointed Laurence King to restore the church; he was an ecclesiastical architect renowned for his sympathetic restoration of church interiors.

So the church today is the fruit of very many peoples' hard work and dedication, in raising the money and determinedly carrying forward the vision. Throughout the re-building the Vicar, Wardens and the PCC refused to compromise or go for second best and as a result have gifted to us a beautiful place of worship with treasures such as the East Window by John Hayward and the neo-baroque pipe organ by Arnold, Williamson and Hyatt; both costly and ambitious projects for their time.

Perhaps the genius of the restoration of S. Mary's is that the interior remains as fresh and bright now as when it was first completed. The Visitors Book records again and again the pleasure and delight of many pilgrims and visitors who are surprised by joy on first entering the church.

This book is dedicated to all those who contributed to the rebuilding of S. Mary & All Saints Church, Little Walsingham, and especially to Father Alan Roe Vicar of the Parish from 1959 - 1977. At a most important time in the history of the village, Walsingham was blessed in having a priest and pastor whose evident faith and love of the Gospel so inspired others that the church was re-built in little over three years. And with such imagination and generosity that it continues to excite and delight as much now as when the doors were reopened in 1964.

And for this thanks be to God.

+ Norman
Richborough

The Rt Revd Norman Aidan Banks
Bishop of Richborough

The Pilgrimage Church of our Lady of Walsingham.

A church, originally dedicated to All Saints, has stood on the present site since Saxon times but nothing now remains older than the 14th century.

Prior to 1921 the church contained two items of particular importance:

- the **Seven Sacrament Font** is probably the finest example to be found in East Anglia. The magnificent font cover, given by Lady Sydney, was destroyed by the fire and the intense heat also caused the pink marks on the stone.

- the **Sidney Tomb** is in memory of Sir Henry and Lady Sidney, who owned the estate from the Reformation until 1638. It was originally in the Chancel but moved to the Guilds, or the north, Chapel of the church in the 1860's. It was badly damaged during the fire and consequently moved to the west end of the church during the building restoration.

Following his appointment as Vicar in 1921, Father Alfred Hope Patten re-established devotion to Our Lady of Walsingham and set up a newly carved image and Shrine in the Guilds Chapel of the church in July 1922. Consequently, the village of Walsingham became again a centre of pilgrimage. The statue of Our Lady was translated to the Holy House in the new Shrine on 15th October 1931.

The Seven Sacrament Font

After the drawing by Hanslip Fletcher
Published by The Medici Society Ltd, London

The Lady Chapel
left and above showing the Sidney Tomb

4

Statue of
Our Lady
situated at
the foot of
the Bell Tower
steps

Saint George's
Altar in the
south aisle

The High Altar

Shrine of
Saint Anthony of Padua

Shrine of
the Sacred Heart

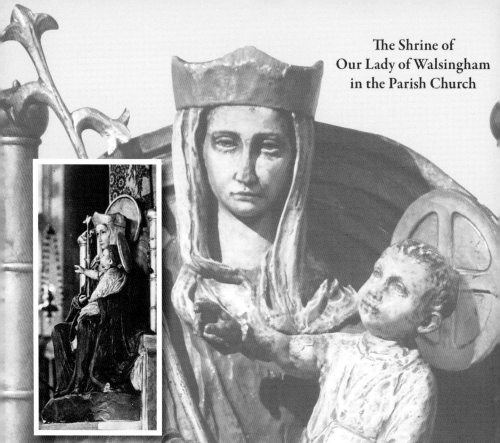

The Shrine of
Our Lady of Walsingham
in the Parish Church

THE SHRINE OF OUR LADY, LITTLE WALSINGHAM.

A postcard of the
Church's Shrine

Parish Ch. Lt. Walsingham
Shrine of Our Lady

A painting by Clifford Pember replaced the
statue of Our Lady of Walsingham, when it
was moved to the new Shrine in 1931. Sadly the
painting was destroyed by the fire.

These dramatic pictures of the fire, and others in this book, are by Ken Faircloth (Photographer, Little Walsingham) and a staff photographer of the Eastern Daily Press.

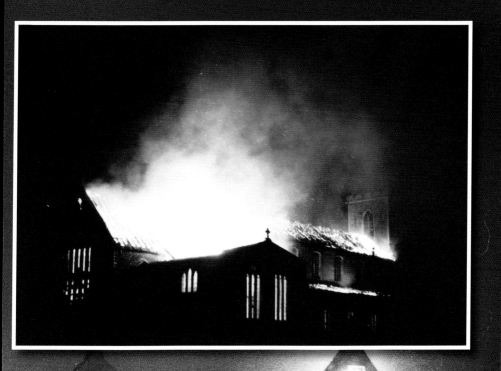

Midnight Alert for Clergy After Two Incidents

NORFOLK CHURCH GUTTED, ANOTHER RANSACKED

Nave of St. Mary's Little Walsingham a Smoking Ruin

WHILE police were investigating a serious case of vandalism in Dereham Parish Church last night, fire swept through St. Mary's Parish Church at Little Walsingham, less than 15 miles away.

The blaze had got a firm hold on the inside of Walsingham Church before the outbreak was noticed. In no time, flames were leaping from the roof on the north side, and the whole of the church was aglow from the mass of fire. It seemed that little or nothing could be done to save many of the precious relics inside.

At Dereham, the church was entered some time after Evensong, and everything that was more capable of being moved was systematically thrashed. Two altars were overturned together with the lectern, and memorial candlesticks were snapped in half.

Linked?

Late last night, in view of what had happened earlier in the evening at Dereham, followed by the Walsingham fire, clergy over a wide area of Norfolk were warned to keep their churches locked.

It was understood that the possibility of a link between the two incidents had been investigated. The police at Walsingham was raised by Mrs. Esra Carter, who lives close by at Walsingham cottage, and her estate agent, Mr. D. Birt, of Wells Road.

An early arrival, Mr. L. B. Whatley, named the church and friend the glass a mass of flames. He and there was nothing anybody could do to rescue anything inside.

Work of Maniac: Dereham Vicar

A STRONG force of Dereham police, headed by Supt. Colin Sidell, were last night investigating an outbreak of vandalism in Dereham Parish Church that was described by the Vicar as "the worst I have ever known."

Whether the vandalism had any deeper significance possible of a religious nature Supt. Sidell said that it was impossible at this stage to say. The possibility, however, could not be ruled out and he was supported in this view by Canon Bowyer.

The damage to the church and its fittings was discovered last night at 8.30 p.m. by Mrs. E. C. Thompson, the sidesman's wife, who was barely seven by road.

In addition no damage seemed to be done to the four candlesticks—one memorial, put glass was worth £200—Canon Bowyer said. Several valuables, including a copper enamelled crucifix and a brass-bound alms chest, survived the rampage.

TERRIBLE

A valuable re-painting was also involved and stains smeared and rent into a heap. There was no sign after night of vandalism.

"A result at terrible. I can only find out what the work of maniacs said. Canon Bowyer.

The Vicar, the Rev. Ewbank, was one of the congregation of St. Nicholas Church this morning and every other church in the district was warned to keep a strict watch.

Several churches in the district are to be patrolled through the night, and police added stations last night.

Two months ago a valuable war driven into Dereham St. Peter and Paul's Church at the weekend and the entered the safe, which obtained money from a collection box.

It was confirmed that these books carried Church notices from the sacred altar. These have since returned unmarked, and one church returned with the message "With the compliments of..."

The church, about seven miles away, was entered about dusk.

(Continued on Page 13)

Timber Roofs

Soon, fire brigades were arriving from different parts of Norfolk, and firemen fought the difficult task of trying to stop the spread of the devastating blaze.

At one time there was danger of the church of being out of control and saving the stone tower. The church, which dates from the 14th century, had a timber roof.

The lovely figures carried by the Sacred of Trinity returning from God first carved and formed from limestone, were saved. Church stone from this stone formed from the church stone from...

(Continued on Page 13)

TRADE GAP SLASHED BY £41m

BRITAIN'S trade gap was slashed last month to £41 million, compared with £82,000,000 in May and £58 million in June last year. Except for April when the gap was £38 million, this figure is the lowest since January, 1960.

Provisional figures issued by the Board of Trade yesterday show that June's imports fell by £19,000,000 (£265,000,000 to £246,000,000) while exports are up (£239,000,000 £245,000,000), and imports fell £40 million (£283,000,000 to £237,000,000).

After eliminating normal seasonal fluctuations, the trade deficit shows the visible trade deficit was greater June less than three months ago and last month from the two previous months.

The main item responsible for this fall in exports from £246,000,000 in May to £237,000,000 last month, was the fall in food supplies over £7 million and tobacco £4 million.

INDUSTRIALISTS ON MARKET ENTRY:
'Narrow the Differences'

AFTER debating British relations with the Common Market, the Federation of British Industries said yesterday that their majority opinion was that Britain should not become committed until differences had been narrowed.

A statement by the Federation's Grand council: "We should greatly welcome an entry and to the fullest possible. Nevertheless a large majority is of the opinion that it is right not to become committed to formal negotiations with Six until existing differences over the problems outlined have been so far narrowed as to offer the prospect of a satisfactory outcome.

After discussing the major issues outstanding, the statement says: "We would not expect to reach agreement in this way in every respect that the Commonwealth was to put a fundamental difficulty in the way of British association with the Common Market."

Kassem's 'War of Attrition' Threat

MR. KASSEM, the Iraqi Prime Minister, last night warned in a "war of attrition" the British if they did not evacuate the British forces in the Kuwait.

General Kassem, in an interview at his palace with foreign correspondents, issued an ultimatum to Britain and said they must withdraw their troops at once.

Kassem said they intended to liberate Kuwait "by all legitimate means" and declared that the British troops still there should get out "sooner or later."

Britain sent forces were for some weeks to help Kuwait after Iraq's threats to seize the oil-rich state. There are now believed to be about 6,000 British servicemen in the area.

Reliably reliable sources yesterday stated that the Iraqi Army was at the border of Kuwait, and a statement would be made at the weekend.

Three Drowned When Car Falls Off Ferry

THREE people were reported drowned last night when a car toppled off a ferry at Leeds Castle.

A woman and two men were drowned and a man, believed to have been the driver proceeded to tumble into water.

Marathon's End

The last Vauxhall Marathon run, with John O'Grady as holder of a non-stop marathon relay to Land's End arrived in dust-devastation at 1.45 p.m. yesterday. That led covered the 896 miles in 120 hours 40 minutes.

Two Lifeboats Out in North Norfolk Rescue

WELLS LIFEBOAT was due in harbour early today with the occupants of the 31-foot cabin cruiser Boy John, which had dragged her anchor and had been drifting off the North Norfolk coast.

Early today the lifeboat called Humber Radio. "We have picked up the casualty and have got him in tow." Proceeding to Wells Harbour and reportedly slowly to O.K."

A "they were expected in harbour

Two People?

It is believed the Boy John left King's Lynn bound for Yarmouth yesterday morning with two people on board.

Earlier both the Sheringham and Wells lifeboats were searching off the coast for the Boy John.

After a day of searches all round the coast, a Cromer radio amateur picked up a "Mayday" message from the cruiser at 1.50 a.m., and the Wells lifeboat went to the rescue. At 2.35 p.m. she was in touch with Mr. Blakeney with her motor boats broken down and needing help. It was not known who was aboard her.

Both Sheringham lifeboat and the Cromer Actify reached the position shortly after 8.50 p.m. but could not find the vessel. They searched for an hour and a half and were back on the beach before midnight.

Sheringham lifeboat was launched at 1.26 p.m. and Wells lifeboat went out at 2.41 p.m. to give assistance.

The Actify was in touch with Sheringham lifeboat helping in the search until shortly after dawn, and also Weaverham, of Hull, was watching for the scene as a small bit the area.

Though the Actify sighted a distress rocket at about 9.50 p.m., she could see nothing of the motor cruiser. The rocket was clearly visible from Sheringham lifeboat.

Cromer coastguards were unable to contact Sheringham lifeboat by radio and asked the Actify to intercept her. The Actify saw the distress signal and reported that no boat could receive her, but was unable to transmit.

Only Link

The distress began when the D. L. Bowling, the Cromer coastguard radio amateur, being an amateur, picked up a distress message from the Boy John, the skipper and his wife were in distress under water with the cruiser, whose passage was passed on to the coastguards by Mr. Bowling.

At 3.00 p.m. he received a message that the Boy John was burning water (at 1.50 p.m. the skipper and his wife) near the Sheringham lifeboat could assist her.

Ten minutes later the coastguards' broadcast another message that the cruiser was then two miles off Blakeney Point.

Later, however, Wells coastguard reported sighting a flare five to six miles north off the coast. It was then believed that the Boy John and another cruiser had left the same port but were in the same area.

Three flares and an S.O.S. on a lamp were rubbed five to six miles off Blakeney at about midnight. A rocket from the cruiser and she was distinguished by the same coastguard who had seen the engine at turn.

Wells lifeboat fired Sheringham lifeboat off the course. At l.45 a.m., the Boy John had been towed by Wells lifeboat and taken off her anchor.

A Cromer motorboat was off guard for Mr. Bowling, who passed

ROAD VICTIM DIES

ANOTHER Norfolk boy died yesterday, George King, of Beaumont whose was a local accident victim St. William's.

He was Gordon Oakes, of 32, Beechwood Drive, Thorpe. The accident also involved a car.

Peace in the Orchard

Underlinings were given in the High Court yesterday to prevent a woman from keeping bees for entering to stray away birds from a neighbouring cherry orchard.

T.U.C. TO REVIEW AFFAIRS OF E.T.U.

A SPECIAL MEETING of the T.U.C. General Council will be held on Monday to consider whether there is any justification for an investigation into the affairs of the Electrical Trades Union, said Mr. George Woodcock, general secretary of the T.U.C., yesterday.

Mr. Woodcock made this statement after meeting Mr. Frank Foulkes, the E.T.U. president, at Congress House, London, for an hour.

Mr. Foulkes was one of the five defendants in the recent High Court case which resulted in Mr. John Byrne being elected deputy secretary of the E.T.U. in place of Mr. F. L. Haxell.

After the meeting, Mr. Woodcock recalled that the General Council had been looking into the affairs of the E.T.U. for about 18 months and they suspended their talks pending the outcome of the court proceedings.

This Wednesday a court ruled that Mr. Byrne who drew an affidavit to actions taken by the Executive Council of the E.T.U. which made consideration at the earliest possible moment of the question of greater militancy. The Woodcock expressed...

NEED FOR SPEED

He said there had been strongly felt he had realised at least that three years could fit Mr. Foulkes.

Mr. Woodcock said that Monday's meeting of the General Council would be asked if they thought there was justification for an inquiry. No representatives of the E.T.U. would be required to attend.

"I am hoping that their interpretation can take place after the normal meetings of the Finance and General Purposes Committee on Monday week. The reason for moving with this speed was the importance of the affidavit in September." he added.

Dealing with the battle between Mr. Haxell and Mr. Byrne, Mr. Byrne served that the union Executive had decided by a majority to kill Mr. Byrne's appointment.

ANGOLA VISIT

Mr. G. Marston Williams, O.B. Assistant Secretary of State for African affairs, will visit Angola to give first hand impressions to Nassau.

NEW MERGER PLAN

British Oxygen Houses, which are primarily a link with a leading American company, have now received proposals for a merger with the British subsidiaries of another big U.S. concern.

SUFFOLK SECOND

Sussex won the county with rifle championship yesterday in the match organised by the English Twenty Club, scoring 1063 out of a possible 1090 to beat Suffolk by two points.

STRIKE SPREADS

Because of an extension of the strike among BOAC maintenance staff at London Airport, there will be more cancellations of services today.

E.L.G.I. HEAD DIES

Lord McGowan, former chairman of Imperial Chemical Industries, has died in a London nursing home aged 87.

Pope's Survey Lays Emphasis on Farming and Aid

A AGRICULTURAL credit policies, ways of curbing the drift from the land, and an increase in overseas and without strings were advocated yesterday by the Pope in an encyclical on social and economic problems.

His letter marks the seventieth anniversary of Pope Leo XIII's "Rerum Novarum" "of new things" which is the Roman Catholic Church's basic document on social and economic problems of the modern world.

The Pope approved birth control and said that, on a worldwide basis, the increase in population was not so great as to justify birth restriction—a point developments and availability of food did not as present, or in the near future, create serious problems.

TECHNOLOGY

The Pope called for "renewed scientific and technical effort so the part of man to master and extend his efforts." He said in science and technology showed no "limitless horizon" and he declared their use to promote "terrible instruments of ruin and death."

Expressing great concern for the state of agriculture and the drift from the land, the Pope called for development of economic systems to ensure that agricultural communities were not left behind by the urban revolution.

All essential services should be developed in country areas and there should be a good system of taxation so that country towns could be well serviced, and run on modern lines. The Pope urged the need for special credit policies and institutions to guarantee to agricultural capital

on the special terms it required. He also approved price protection for agricultural products and the collaboration of agricultural cooperatives which could also take part in political movements.

The Pope further welcomes provided in negative aspects which restricted human freedom and personal initiative were curbed while preventing the individual's right to private property and that his individual distinctions among men should not be wide.

He expressed approval of control by State and public agencies over

on the special terms it required. The also approved price protection for agricultural products and the collaboration of agricultural cooperatives which could also take part in political movements.

POPE JOHN'S encyclical urges:—

- Techniques to increase man's output.
- Modern services in country areas to combat drift from the land.
- Special credit policies for agriculture.
- Aid for backward countries with starving a colonialism of wealth.

WORLD AID

The Pope called for "politically disinterested aid" and warned such that countries from accepting a new colonialism" by trying to aid to the fundamental of the Church to denounce the under-developed lands and denied help.

To the under-developed lands he gave the advice that their own people and their resources would be better developed before relying on help from abroad.

Pope John's letter is likely to establish itself as one of the great pronouncements of the church and its have wide influence on Catholic communities throughout the world.

NORFOLK CHURCH GUTTED, ANOTHER RANSACKED

Nave of St. Mary's
Little Walsingham
a Smoking Ruin

WHILE police were investigating a serious case of vandalism in Dereham Parish Church last night, fire swept through St. Mary's Parish Church at Little Walsingham, less than 15 miles away.

The blaze had got a firm hold on the inside of Walsingham Church before the outbreak was noticed. In no time, flames were leaping from the roof on the north side, and the whole of the church was aglow from the mass of fire. It seemed that little or nothing could be done to save many of the precious relics inside.

At Dereham, the church was entered some time after Evensong, and everything that was capable of being moved was systematically smashed. Two altars were overturned together with the lectern, and memorial candlesticks were snapped in half.

Linked?

Late last night, in view of what had happened earlier in the evening at Dereham, followed by the Walsingham fire, clergy over a wide area of Norfolk were warned to keep their churches locked.

It was understood that the possibility of a link between the two incidents had not been discounted.

The alarm at Walsingham was raised by Mrs. John Gurney, who lives close by at Walsingham Abbey, and her estate agent, Mr. D. Hoy, at once put through a call to the brigade.

An early arrival, Mr. L .H. Whitmore, opened the church door and found the place a mass of flames. He said there was nothing anybody could do to rescue anything inside.

Timber Roofs

Soon, fire brigades were arriving from different parts of Norfolk, and firemen tackled the difficult task of trying to save part of the building. At one time there was danger of the steeple collapsing and the crowd was warned to stand well away.

The church, mainly in the Perpendicular style, had fine open timber roofs.

It contained the finest Seven Sacrament font in England, with a well carved Classic cover. There was a carved screen to the south transept and some miserere seats in the chancel.

The church, which dated from 1558, had some ancient stained glass.

A reporter who stood with a crowd of villagers watched the church blazing from one end to the other with flames roaring along the length of the church roof and the figures of firemen perched on their ladders, directing the hoses into the inferno.

Yet at 11 p.m. the hours rang out from the clock in the church tower as if nothing were happening.

By 11.30 p.m., the flames had been virtually extinguished by the firemen, who had come from Wells and Fakenham, and they were warning people not to approach too closely to the church entrance because of a danger from the bells in the tower.

Font Safe

A reporter, who was able to get a glimpse inside the church, found it was a tangled mess of ruin, with smoke still pouring from the heaps of debris lying all over the floor. Hardly any of the normal features of the church could be recognised through the haze of smoke.

In front was the historic font, which had apparently withstood the fire, though it seemed evident that the wooden cover had been severely damaged.

The Vicar, the Rev. A. A. Roe, was apparently away at the time. The Administrator of the Shrine Church, Father Colin Stephenson told the Press that it was a great catastrophe, but, he added, "The church will rise again."

At 1.30 a.m. firemen were still inside the church pouring water on to the smoking ruin in the light of the fire brigade's searchlights.

The Father Hope Patten Memorial Chapel, which is upstairs over the south porch, had escaped damage, but the rest of the church is in ruin.

The church documents were in a safe inside the church and no attempt had been made to open the safe early today. The pews were all charred and virtually destroyed.

It is understood that the church doors had been locked after the service.

Walsingham Blaze

(Continued from Page 1)

of villagers watched the church blazing from one end to the other with flames roaring along the length of the church roof and the figures of firemen perched on their ladders, directing the hoses into the inferno.

Yet at 11 p.m. the hours rang out from the clock in the church tower as if nothing were happening.

By 11.30 p.m. the flames had been virtually extinguished by the firemen, who had come from Wells and Fakenham, and they were warning people not to approach too closely to the church entrance because of a danger from the bells in the tower.

Font Safe

A reporter, who was able to get a glimpse inside the church, found it was a tangled mess of ruin, with smoke still pouring from the heaps of debris lying all over the floor. Hardly any of the normal features of the church could be recognised through the haze of smoke.

In front was the historic font, which had apparently withstood the fire, though it seemed evident that the wooden cover had been severely damaged.

The Vicar, the Rev. A. A. Roe, was apparently away at the time. The Administrator of the Shrine Church, Father Colin Stephenson, told the Press that it was a great catastrophe, but, he added, "The church will rise again."

At 1.30 a.m. firemen were still inside the church pouring water on to the smoking ruin in the light of the fire brigade's searchlights.

The Father Hope Patten Memorial Chapel, which is upstairs over the south porch, had escaped damage, but the rest of the church is in ruin.

The church documents were in a safe inside the church and no attempt had been made to open the safe early today. The pews were all charred and virtually destroyed.

It is understood that the church doors had been locked after the service.

Flames sweeping through the inside of Little Walsingham Church at the height of the blaze.

13

MEMORIES OF THE FIRE

An article written by *The Revd Colin Stephenson* and first published in the Walsingham Review No.2 September 1961.

"On the afternoon of July 14th, I went at 3 p.m. to hear confessions at St Mary's as the Vicar was away. Afterwards, because it was raining, I sat quietly for a while in the church remembering the impression it made on me when I first saw it and wondering whether it still made the same impact on those who for the first time stand beside the magnificent font and look down its great length and experienced the almost indescribable feeling of holiness and antiquity. I little thought that I was saying good-bye to the St Mary's known, loved and worshipped in by so many people all over the world, and the historic spot where in 1922 the pilgrimage to Our Lady of Walsingham was re-established. Only a week before the village people had come to a Sung Mass to commemorate the setting up of the image in their parish church and I administered the Chalice, and then myself said Mass in the Guilds Chapel where there were still many signs of those memorable years when the Shrine of Our Lady of Walsingham had been venerated upon the pillar where, after the Holy House had been rebuilt, an icon was set in fulfilment of Fr Patten's promise to the Bishop that he would not place another image there.

That evening when I retired to bed soon after 10 p.m. my telephone rang and it was the Reverend Mother to say that there seemed to be a fire somewhere as they could see a red glow from the convent, and as she was afraid there might be people in trouble or even injured, she asked whether she should send a Sister to find out where the fire was. I said I had better get up in case anyone needed the Sacraments. I went to the window and by this time it was obvious that there was a big fire and I was afraid it was the Abbey which was burning, but almost immediately the phone rang again and Reverend Mother in great distress told me that St Mary's was alight.

I hurried down the Village Street where there was a feeling of crisis and the whole village was awake, and some already were in tears. I could smell the burning as I approached, and then as I turned the corner into Church Street, I could see the flames devouring this ancient and lovely building. The firemen were fighting gallantly to save the tower and spire which they did entirely through their determined efforts; but it was not until I went along the Sunk Road and looked at the church from that exciting side view, from which it has always impressed me with its great length, that I was able to see the full horror of the fire, and I was there when the roof fell in with a sickening sound. Throughout it all the old clock struck out the quarters as though nothing was happening. Obviously the organ must have caught alight, how we shall probably never know, but this carried the flames to the roof. By the time it was discovered the whole building was an inferno of flame, so that it was impossible to save anything. Next day the Tabernacle was dug out of the ruins, but the Holy Sacrament had been consumed by the fire. There was nothing one could do but stand and watch it burn, and it was an experience of such horror that my feelings just simply could not react to it; and I just felt dead and empty. In fact, next morning when I awoke I wondered whether the whole thing had been a dream it had so much the quality of a nightmare, but the ruins were there and a sorry sight they are. I do not believe that anyone who did not know St Mary's could possibly imagine what it was like from what now remains, and however it may be rebuilt, I am sure we shall always be grateful that we knew the old St Mary's; and the words which kept ringing in my ears that night and since are those with which Holy Week makes us familiar: -

> "Our holy and beautiful house where our fathers praised
> Thee is burned up with fire: and all our pleasant things laid waste."

Father Dominic Pyle-Bridges recalls:

"I was one of three servers at the very last service, Benediction of the Blessed Sacrament, in St Mary's before the fire.

After we returned to the Hospice, Michael Farrer (who later became Founder and First Secretary of the Anglo Catholic History Society) came in and said that "something was up". We made our way at speed, with others, and indeed something was up - St Mary's was in flames. We stood in Sunk Road watching the fire when suddenly a church bell started tolling! Obviously it was the heat causing the bell to ring but the bell tolled with a regularity as if for a funeral - as indeed it was. We must have been there for several hours but, as we often said in later years, it was as if all was in slow motion. The moment came when the roof opened and the flames went so very high and then with a crash the roof fell in.

Shortly after this we went back to our lodgings where hot drinks had been made. I phoned my mother and told her and she wept at such appalling news.

The following day the smell of smoke, wet ash and something that could not be defined permeated the whole village.

We walked back to the church and took some photographs and I picked up a piece of burnt wood from the north door to keep as a memento. Such a simple item can still revive very strong memories and I am glad that I can remember the old St Mary's with all its history."

Betty Howe,
former Walsingham Postmistress and first lady Churchwarden of St Mary's, recalls:

"I'd been playing Bingo in the Parish Hall in Friday Market and was just on my way home when someone called out "The church is on fire!". First I ran home to the Post Office to tell my parents the news and then I ran from the High Street to Church Street as far as the bridge; nobody was allowed beyond this point. Firemen and police were already at the church and the fire hoses were being directed at the church tower and spire. There was great concern the tower would collapse.

Like all the other people who were there I could only stand and stare - I couldn't believe it! I didn't want to believe it and after a short while I decided I couldn't stand there any longer and watch the church disappear so I returned home.

"...... the fire sorted out the death watch beetle!"

The following morning I was up early as usual to start work in the Post Office but decided not to go round to the church again that day or for some time.

Sunday services were then held at St Peter's, Great Walsingham. My mother and I attended the service, in May 1962, in the ruins of St Mary's to mark the beginning of the re-building. We were all delighted with the news the church was to be rebuilt because the idea of not doing so was never an option as far as I was concerned!

The old church needed repairs and improvements. So the fire brought many changes. The roof was in bad need of repair and the fire sorted out the death watch beetle!

The impact of the fire on the village was very great, not least on Fr Alan Roe. He had been Vicar for barely two years before the fire and spent a lot of time on pastoral care including visiting the sick and house-bound. He now found himself facing the same task as a predecessor, Fr Hope Patten, - to raise funds! Fr Roe succeeded and the church was re-built in just over three years and re-consecrated in August 1964."

Geoffrey Tuck
former Walsingham Postman, 1960 - 1994, recalls:

"I'm a Wells man, born and bred, and spent many years working on steam trains before moving to Walsingham in 1955.

On 14th July 1961, I was having a quiet birthday drink with some friends in the Black Lion in Friday Market. Tubby Frary, who was cowman at Abbey Farm, looked out of the window and saw a glow in the sky. He thought the farm was on fire so we all put down our glasses and ran down Church Street towards the farm.

The smell of smoke and glow in the sky increased as we ran but we were stopped at the bridge by the police and then we realised it was the church, not the farm, on fire. There were many police and firemen at the church gates and they seemed to be concentrating on controlling the fire in the church tower because they were worried the tower would fall on Church House, the home of the Walsingham Estate Agent, Mr Hoy.

"I was having a quiet birthday drink ......"

We could only stand and watch what was happening. Crowds of people were gathering around the church, in Sunk Road, up by the farm house and with us at the bridge in Church Street. There was nothing we could do but only look at the church which stood out in the darkness.

Eventually, I'm not sure what the time was, I went home because I had to get up early for work in the morning but I never went back to the Black Lion to finish my drink!

On Saturday morning I arrived at the Post Office and noticed there were still a lot of people in the village the morning after the fire. Betty Howe and I talked about the events of the night before as we sorted the mail and filled my post sack. The smell of the fire hung around for a very long time.

Over the next few years I got to know the Lusher's [the builder's] workmen, who were re-building the church, quite well as I cycled past the church every day.

I was married in St Mary's in 1957 and got to know Fr Roe quite well, because I saw him daily as his Postman. He was a real village person and got around a lot. More than that he, with the help of others, got the church rebuilt."

Roy & Veronica Howard (née Wright) recall:

"Following a village cricket team practice, my boy friend, Roy, had cycled from Hindringham to my home in Church Street, close to the church, to see me. He had returned home via Sunk Road at approximately 8 p.m. and had seen nothing wrong at the church.

Later I had been knitting with my mother while my father had been decorating another room with a friend. Suddenly I heard people running outside and shouting 'the church is on fire!' I went out and joined people at the bridge in Church Street and watched the firemen fighting the fire near to the church tower. They were afraid the tower would collapse. My father went to Church House and retrieved Mr Hoy's dog and budgie but I could only stand and watch the fire in disbelief.

On Saturday morning it was as if Friday evening had all been an awful dream. A strange smell of burning lingered in the air and I couldn't believe the church had been destroyed.

My early years had very much been centred around St Mary's, having been baptised and confirmed there. It was customary in my day for candidates for Confirmation to be confirmed on a Thursday or Friday, make their Confession on Saturday and then receive their first Communion on Sunday.

I also remember the important and loving role played by the Sisters from the Priory and their work with the children.

I often took part in the tradition of young girls of the village wearing white and preceding the statue of Our Lady of Walsingham in processions around the village.

We were both delighted the church was restored in a remarkably short time and we were able to be married in St Mary's, following the re-consecration, in 1965.

Out of the devastation of the fire emerged a wonderful new church."

J. Barrie Wells recalls:

"I joined St Mary's choir at 8 years of age and became a server when my voice broke. I have many memories of being trained as a server by Stanley Smith and serving for Fr Hope Patten in both black and red cassocks.

On the evening of 14th July I had not long returned home, after a very long journey on my Lambretta, and was ready for bed. Suddenly my aunt called out the church was on fire and from the back of the house I could see a red glow in the sky. I got dressed again and ran from the High Street to the church steps where the firemen were directing their hoses on the tower and west end of the church. Doubtless because so much water was hosed on this area there was comparatively little damage to the tower; in fact, only one beam was damaged!

St Hugh's Chapel, above the south porch, was not damaged due to its spiral staircase and the amount of water sprayed over its roof although it was very, very sooty and smokey when we eventually went inside.

Like other people who had arrived on the scene, I could only stand and stare and watch the firemen for most of the night. There was nothing I could do. Sometime after midnight I went home for a few hours sleep.

Early the following morning, Len Whitmore (the Shrine's Beadle) and I, with some other people, were allowed into the church to check if anything of value had survived the fire. The Sacristy was in the south-east corner of the church and the first thing we found were the brass candlesticks which were in pieces because the metal solder had melted. The cast iron record box was intact but inside the vellum covered records now appeared to be covered in jelly!

Len Whitmore managed to retrieve the Reserved Sacrament Tabernacle from the High Altar but when it was opened later, by a priest, it was discovered all the contents had been consumed by the fire. After a long day I went home tired and very sooty.

The firemen told Len and I the fire appeared to have started in three places - the Sacristy, the choir vestry in the north-west corner and the Lady Chapel. The flames had been seen through the Lady Chapel window by a passer-by who raised the alarm. Obviously the reported three seats of the fire gave rise to the suspicion of arson.

Fr Roe was on holiday at the time of the fire but was called back to Walsingham with the message 'your church has been raised to the ground!'.

I visited the church many times during the period of reconstruction, often with Fr Roe who was a caring parish priest determined to get the church restored. I continued to serve him until he retired sadly on the grounds of ill health."

The Revd Alan Roe,
Vicar of Walsingham &
The Rt Revd Launcelot Fleming
Bishop of Norwich

Eastern Daily Press

SATURDAY, JANUARY 20, 1962

Weather—Rain in Places Later

Walsingham Church Restored by Mid 1963?

ST. MARY'S CHURCH, Little Walsingham, gutted by fire last year, may be completely restored by the early summer of 1963.

But more money is needed and the appeal to the public for contributors continues.

Out to Tender

The work will go out to tender and the Vicar, the Rev. A. A. Bee said last night: "We hope to make a start in the spring."

Furnishings

The ruins of St. Mary's Church, Little Walsingham, gutted by fire last July. Now that the authorities have received £48,625 from insurance, rebuilding is expected to start in the spring.

from The Eastern Daily Press - 20th January 1962

Walsingham Church Restored by Mid 1963?

ST. MARY'S CHURCH, Little Walsingham, gutted by fire last year, may be completely restored by the early summer of 1963.

But more money is needed and the appeal to the public for contributions continues.

Insurance money received for the church building totals £48,625 and plans for a new church to be built on the same site are now in an advanced stage.

Out to Tender

The work will go out to tender and the Vicar, the Rev. A. A. Roe, said last night, "We hope to make a start in the spring." He mentioned May 1st as a possible date.

The response to the general appeal which followed the devastation by fire has yielded £4,500. Money is still coming in. The Vicar said he was still receiving money from Episcopalians in America, many of whom had visited Walsingham.

He added, "We will build on the old foundation and outwardly the church will look the same."

Furnishings

It is expected the work will take a year to complete.

Insurance money for the interior furnishings has not yet been received and negotiations over it are continuing.

The Vicar said, "I think we have done pretty well. I hope it will be ready to go out to tender in March."

from a Parish Leaflet

ST. MARY'S PARISH CHURCH, WALSINGHAM

This picture gives an idea of the nearly complete destruction of the Church during the night of Friday, July 14th. Only the tower and some walls are left standing.

The cause of the Fire is still unknown.

Work is already under way to make the remains safe, and it is hoped to sing Mass in the ruins on the Sunday after the Assumption, if safe and weather permitting. The Parish continues to worship in St. Peter's and in the Shrine.

Can you PLEASE help in the RESTORATION by sending a DONATION

To Fr. ROE at Walsingham Vicarage.

from The Eastern Daily Press - May 1962

Service in Ruined Church

From an improvised altar, the Vicar of Walsingham, the Rev. A. A. Roe, conducts a service in the ruins of St. Mary's Church, Little Walsingham. The church was gutted by fire last year and the service, held yesterday, was a special one to mark the beginning of restoration work.

In effect it was an open air service for the church has no roof, or windows. Work began immediately the service was over.

The Vicar told a reporter afterwards that he expected the restoration to be completed in 15 to 18 months. A sum of £15,000 was still required. The contractors had been able to employ a few local men and work would begin in real earnest on Monday.

There was a large congregation for the service including clergy from the district and representatives of the builders and the firm of architects.

The building restoration was undertaken by
W. S. Lusher & Son of Norwich under the
direction of **Laurence King** FRIBA, Architect

Dereham & Fakenham Times
The Norfolk Chronicle and Journal

FRIDAY, MAY 10, 196.   THREEP:

Friday 10th May 1963

Walsingham Church rebuilding

The photograph shows progress made with the rebuilding of the Church of St. Mary and All Saints, Walsingham, which was destroyed by fire on July 14th, 1961. The church is to be rebuilt in its original 14th-century form at a cost of £82,000.

The Vicar (the Rev. A. A. Roe) said this week that about £13,000 was still required. He hoped the work would be completed by the beginning of November, though the organ would not be finished by then.

CONSECRATION

THIS CHURCH WHICH WAS DESTROYED BY FIRE ON
14th JULY 1961 WAS RECONSECRATED BY THE LORD
BISHOP OF NORWICH ON SATURDAY 8th AUGUST 1964
AFTER HAVING BEEN REBUILT BY W. S. LUSHER & SON
BUILDERS OF NORWICH UNDER THE DIRECTION OF
LAURENCE KING F.R.I.B.A. ARCHITECT
VICAR THE REV. A. A. ROE
CHURCHWARDENS
JOHN BANSON · ROBIN SAYER

"GOOD people, by virtue of our sacred office in the Church of God, we do now declare to be consecrate, and for ever set apart from profane, common and ordinary uses this House of God, under the dedication of the Blessed Mary ever-Virgin Mother of God and All Saints. In the Name of the Father and of the Son and of the Holy Ghost. AMEN."

The Rt Revd Launcelot Fleming ~ Bishop of Norwich

SAINT MARY AND ALL SAINTS
WALSINGHAM

CONSECRATION
of the
RESTORED CHURCH

SATURDAY, 8th AUGUST, 1964
at 3.0 p.m.

CHURCH TIMES

No. 5,296.—Vol. CXLVII   LONDON, FRIDAY, AUGUST 14, 1964   (Registered at the G.P.O. as a newspaper)   PRICE 5d.

WALSINGHAM CEREMONY

The Bishop of Norwich is handed the petition to reconsecrate the restored St. Mary's, Walsingham. See story on back page

The Bishop of Norwich
is handed the petition
to reconsecrate
the restored
St. Mary's
by the Vicar,
the Revd A. A. Roe

The Bishop of Norwich
with
Fr Michael Smith
(South Creake)
& Fr Michael McLean

30

from The Journal, Friday August 14, 1964
BEFORE consecrating the restored Church of St Mary and All Saints, Walsingham, the Bishop of Norwich (Dr. Launcelot Fleming), who is to be seen in the centre of this procession, sprinkled holy water on the outer walls.

GUARDIANS of the Anglican Shrine approach the church, led by the Beadle (Mr. L. Whitmore) and Fr. Colin Stephenson, Administrator of the Shrine.

LYNN NEWS & ADVERTISER

Postage 5d.   No. 12,898   TUESDAY, AUGUST 11, 1964   Telephone 2092   FOURPENCE

RESTORED CHURCH: TWO BISHOPS IN CEREMONY

JUST THREE YEARS after a raging fire reduced it to a charred ruin, the re-built church of St. Mary and All Saints at Little Walsingham was on Saturday reconsecrated by the Bishop of Norwich, the Rt. Rev. W. L. S. Fleming, helped by the Bishop of Lynn, the Rt. Rev. W. S. Llewellyn.

Over 500 people, including parishioners, clergy and well-wishers from all over the country and abroad, turned into the glowing new interior of the church to watch the cere-

RE-CONSECRATION CEREMONY

THE BISHOP of Norwich, the Rt. Rev. W. L. S. Fleming, blessed the font during Saturday's reconsecration service at Little Walsingham parish church, which was gutted by fire three years ago and has since been re-built at a cost of £65,000.   (CIC 6130)

Eastern Daily Press

MONDAY, AUGUST 10, 1964

The restored nave of Walsingham Parish Church during yesterday's service.

The Organ

The organ in the chancel perished in the fire and the new organ specification was devised by a former organist of the church, Kenneth Condon, in

consultation with the organ builders, Cedric Arnold, Williamson & Hyatt of Essex. The work was completed in 1964 and the organ is now considered to be 'an undisputed masterpiece'.

The Bells

When the tower was built, probably in the 14th century, it was fitted with an oak frame for a ring of four bells. The earliest record of the bells dates from 1539 when *"the parishioners purchased the 'great bell of the late Friars Minor' for use in the parish church"*. In 1552 there were four bells of 12 cwt, 14 cwt, 17 cwt and 21 cwt - an impressively heavy set by local standards. In 1569 the old framework was extended to accommodate a new treble bell but no further work had taken place since the 18th century.

The bells survived the fire. However, they were removed from the tower in

1985, together with the timbers of the old bell-frame, and a new cast-iron and steel frame designed to hold six bells was built into the tower in the same year. The work of restoration was carried out at the Whitechapel Bell Foundry. The five bells were replaced and rededicated in 1987 and a sixth, new treble bell, was cast, hung and dedicated in 1988.

The new treble bell inscription is:

WALSINGHAM PARVA
NOVEMBER 19ᵀᴴ ANNO DOMINI 1987
ALAN HUGHES MADE ME

MY NAME IS FRANCIS
LOUD I'LL RING
FOR MARY
MOTHER OF MY KING

PARISH CHURCH OF ST. MARY
AND ALL SAINTS,
WALSINGHAM

THE HALLOWING OF THE
NEW TREBLE BELL
by The Rt. Revd.
C.L.P. Bishop
Sunday February 14th
1988

After the Homily, The Litany is begun :

Let us pray

God the Father
HAVE MERCY ON US
God the Son
HAVE MERCY ON US
God the Holy Spirit
HAVE MERCY ON US
Holy, blessed and glorious Trinity,
HAVE MERCY ON US

The Parish Church of
St. Mary and all Saints
Walsingham

A
SERVICE OF THANKSGIVING
FOR THE RESTORATION
AND REHANGING
OF THE TOWER BELLS

With their rededication by
The Rt. Revd. Peter Nott
Bishop of Norwich

Sunday 9th August 1987
at 3.30 pm

Saint Hugh
of Lincoln

The pink colouration on the
font stonework was caused by
the intense heat of the fire.

The Sidney Tomb

Seven Sacrament Font

Statue of
Our Lady of
Walsingham
at the site of
the original
Shrine

The
Guilds
Chapel

Saint
Joseph

Saint
Anthony
of Padua

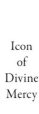

Icon
of
Divine
Mercy

Shrine
of the
Sacred
Heart

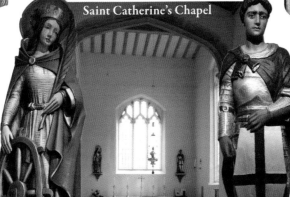

Saint Catherine's Chapel

Saint Catherine
donated by Laurence King - Architect

Saint George
the only statue to survive the fire

36

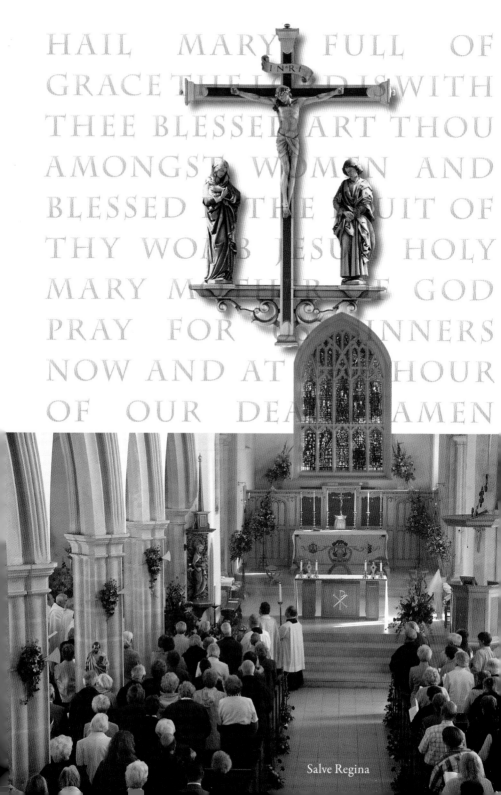

Salve Regina